LAMENESS

by
Stuart Duncan, BVMS, CertEP, MRCVS

Illustrations by
Carole Vincer

KENILWORTH PRESS

First published in Great Britain by
Kenilworth Press, an imprint of Quiller Publishing Ltd

British Library Cataloguing in Publication Data
A catalogue record for this book is available from the British Library

ISBN 978-1-905693-07-8

Printed in Great Britain by Halstan & Co. Ltd

Disclaimer of Liability
This book is not intended as a substitute for the medical advice of a
veterinary surgeon. The author and publisher shall have neither
liability nor responsibility to any person or entity with respect to any
loss or damage caused or alleged to be caused directly or indirectly by
the information contained in this book. While the book is as accurate
as the author can make it, there may be errors, omissions and
inaccuracies.

KENILWORTH PRESS
An imprint of Quiller Publishing Ltd
Wykey House, Wykey, Shrewsbury, SY4 1JA
tel: 01939 261616 fax: 01939 261606
e-mail: info@quillerbooks.com
website: www.kenilworthpress.co.uk

CONTENTS

LAMENESS

4 Introduction
5 Lameness and how to spot it
6 Conformation and foot balance
8 Which is the lame leg?
10 When to call the vet
11 Trotting up for inspection
12 Lameness grading and diagnostic techniques
14 Foot problems
15 Foot abscesses
16 Bruised feet and corns
17 Shoeing-related problems
18 Splints and bone spavin
19 Ringbone and wounds
20 Tendon and ligament injuries
21 Laminitis
22 Muscle problems
23 Preventing lameness
24 Box rest

INTRODUCTION

Most horses and ponies are kept for the purpose of riding, whether for occasional pleasure riding or more demanding equestrian pursuits such as eventing, dressage and racing. Whatever their intended use, lameness is the greatest contributor to loss of equine performance and lost riding and training days.

Equine vets encounter lameness problems on a daily basis, with causes ranging from ill-fitting shoes, strained ligaments and tendons, cuts and infections, to fractures. The aim of this book is to help readers understand the basics of lameness examination and evaluation, as well as to describe some of the more commonly encountered problems.

Initially, it helps to have some appreciation of the basic structure and anatomy of the limbs and feet.

UNEXPLAINED LAMENESS

In most cases a lameness diagnosis can be arrived at through careful clinical examination and imaging techniques. However, even with the advent of advanced imaging, a diagnosis is not always achieved.

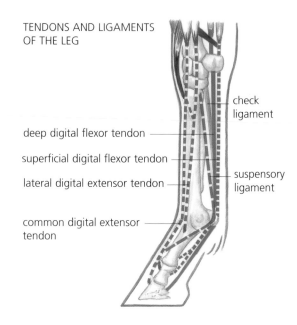

TENDONS AND LIGAMENTS OF THE LEG

check ligament

deep digital flexor tendon

superficial digital flexor tendon

lateral digital extensor tendon

suspensory ligament

common digital extensor tendon

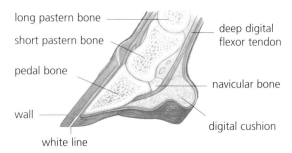

SECTION THROUGH CENTRE OF FOOT

long pastern bone

short pastern bone

pedal bone

wall

white line

deep digital flexor tendon

navicular bone

digital cushion

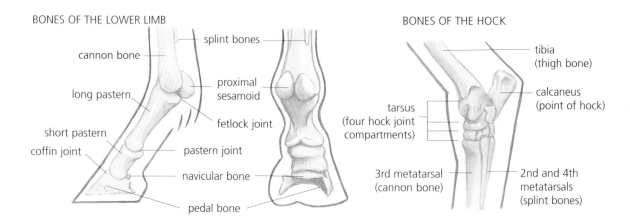

BONES OF THE LOWER LIMB

splint bones

cannon bone

long pastern

short pastern

coffin joint

proximal sesamoid

fetlock joint

pastern joint

navicular bone

pedal bone

BONES OF THE HOCK

tibia (thigh bone)

calcaneus (point of hock)

tarsus (four hock joint compartments)

3rd metatarsal (cannon bone)

2nd and 4th metatarsals (splint bones)

LAMENESS AND HOW TO SPOT IT

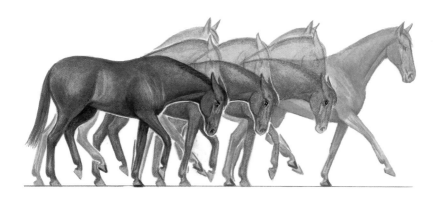

Lameness can be described as a combination of signs such as pain, inflammation or a mechanical defect, which may result in a change in your horse's normal gait. This may show itself as limping or difficulty in walking, trotting or cantering.

When checking for lameness, it is generally best to start with the foot, and work your way up the leg towards the shoulder. Signs which may be associated with lameness include swelling, heat or pain on touch in the lame leg. If there is any doubt as to the significance of these signs, compare them with the opposite leg to get an accurate comparison.

If your horse or pony's lameness is slight when trotted, there may be no head nodding (see page 8) seen. However, if you look carefully and compare one leg against the other, you may be able to spot a difference in the flight pattern of the lame leg, when compared to the normal leg. Some forms of lameness may be more obvious when the horse is going up or down a hill. It is also worth checking the legs for any marks, particularly on the inside of the fetlocks or the heels, which might indicate brushing or forging.

Watch your horse's posture carefully while he is standing quietly in the field or in the stable. He may point the lame foreleg or continually rest the lame hind leg.

Generally, up to 95% of lameness problems occur at the level of the knee or below, and the majority of these originate in the foot.

Some horses and ponies show more than one site of lameness. However, one area of pain is usually more obvious and the main cause of the lameness itself. **Compensatory lameness** (secondary lameness) can develop, for example when a horse attempts to protect the primary source of pain. **Diagonal lameness** can occur in some horses, for instance a primary lameness in the left hock may produce a compensatory lameness in the right front high suspensory ligament through increased loading.

Forelimb lameness is more common than **hind limb lameness** since a horse's centre of gravity, which is dictated by its conformation, is located closer to the forelimbs than to the hind limbs. Trying to recognise hind limb lameness is more difficult; however, a large proportion of hind limb lamenesses are confined to the lower limb including the foot, fetlock and hock.

CONFORMATION AND FOOT BALANCE

Conformation of the lower limb and, to a lesser extent, the overall body itself may play a major role in the development of forelimb and hind limb lameness. Some well-recognised conformational faults may lead directly to lameness problems. Examples of these may be seen in foals and yearlings involving the knee where there is a deviation between the lower and upper limb. Some youngsters may appear 'back at the knee' or have offset knees and these can be important factors in causing lameness.

In the hind limbs, conformationally straight hind limbs or sickle hocks may lead to certain predictable lameness conditions. Evaluation of conformation is therefore an important part of lameness examination.

Gait abnormalities may exist with or without obvious lameness. Examples of such conditions include stringhalt, intermittent upward fixation of the patella (locked stifle) and shivering. Some cases can present without any obvious lameness, however they may complicate the diagnosis if there is an underlying, pre-existing lameness problem. 'Tying up' involving the muscles of the back and pelvis may only result in stiffness in many cases, rather than overt lameness. However, it can cause poor performance in competition horses.

Diagrams showing the use of lines to evaluate normal, straight limb conformation from different perspectives. Vertical lines can be visualised from the front and side of the forelimb as well as from the back and side of the hind limb.

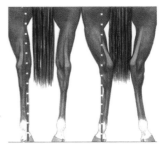

BOW LEGS Both hocks are outside the plumb line. This is commonly seen in young foals.

COW HOCKS Hocks rotated inwards, bringing the points of both hocks closer together. Usually seen in combination with toed-out conformation.

BASE WIDE

Forelimbs outside imaginary plumb line. May or may not be toed in or toed out.

BASE NARROW

Horses stand with forelimbs inside the plumb line and overload the outside of the lower limbs.

NORMAL FORE

Normal forelimb, from the side.

BACK AT THE KNEE

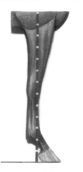

Knee and lower limb are behind the line and are prone to knee-related lameness.

NORMAL HIND

Side view of normal hock.

SICKLE HOCK

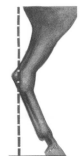

A common fault; may lead to hock lameness as well as tendon or ligament injuries.

ABNORMALITIES OF GAIT

DISHING

Lower limb moves in
a circular fashion;
mainly seen in trot.

FORGING

OVERREACHING

WINGING

BRUSHING

Whole limb shows an
outwardly circular
movement.

A fore or hind foot interferes
with the opposite inside fetlock
or pastern, often resulting in
small injuries.

The conformation of the foot, in particular, is related to lameness. Horses with poor hoof balance may be more susceptible to traumatic foot injuries, including joint, ligament and other soft-tissue problems. **Foot balance** can be assessed in two different planes:

1. The hoof/pastern axis: The hoof/pastern axis is an imaginary straight line from the centre of the fetlock joint through the pastern bone and finishing in the centre of the hoof. Any deviation from this line suggests a broken back (or broken forward) hoof/pastern axis and a possible predisposition to lameness.

2. Medio-lateral balance: This refers to the balance between the inside and the outside of your horse's foot. To check this, pick up his foot and hold it loosely round the cannon, allowing the foot to hang. Imagine two lines, one running straight down the length of the limb and the other at 90° across the back part of the foot. This will highlight discrepancies – whether one side is higher or lower.

Check how your horse's feet hit the ground when walked on a smooth, level, concrete surface in hand. **The heel should contact the ground first, followed by the toe, and the inside and outside parts of the foot should hit the ground together.**

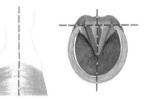

MEDIO-LATERAL BALANCE

HOOF/PASTERN AXIS

A horse with good conformation should have a plumb line down the centre of the limb, bisecting the foot in two equal halves. A line running from the middle of the fetlock at an angle through the coronary band to the hoof bearing surface should be parallel to an imaginary line down the front of the hoof wall and the heel.

A simple metal T-square can be used to accurately assess the medio-lateral balance of the foot. It is held down the back of the limb so that the straight T-piece runs across the back of the heels. It allows you to accurately assess the level of the heels and coronary band.

7

WHICH IS THE LAME LEG?

How to spot front leg lameness

When a sound horse is trotting in a straight line on a firm, level surface the head remains level and the flight pattern of both forelegs is equal. When lameness is present, **the head is raised when the lame leg hits the ground and drops when the sound leg comes into contact with the ground.**

Sometimes it can be difficult to determine which is the lame leg and occasionally lameness may be present in both front limbs. If the lameness is originating from the foot, your horse may 'point his toe' or even hold the affected front leg out in front of him, in order to relieve pressure and weight to the painful area. Shifting from one foreleg to the other may indicate pain (and lameness) in both front legs, for example in cases of laminitis where both front feet are affected, or in cases of tendonitis where there is inflammation in both front leg tendons. In an attempt to alleviate pain from one particular foot, some horses may try to stack bedding under the heels to adopt a toe-down position, particularly if there is pain in the back of the foot, e.g. sore heel syndrome, 'palmar foot pain' or navicular syndrome.

If a horse is suffering from a shoulder injury he may stand with the affected forelimb held back, and when asked to walk forward may drag the affected limb.

Neck pain can be very difficult to diagnose. However, when the horse moves, his head will be kept very high and he may be reluctant to eat food from the ground or to graze.

If lame on a foreleg, the head is raised when the lame leg hits the ground and drops when the sound leg comes into contact with the ground. The horse above is lame on his near fore.

If sound in trot, the flight pattern of both forelegs will be even.

If lameness stems from the foot, the horse may shift his weight from one leg to the other, 'point his toe' or even hold the affected front leg out in front of him. Could be indicative of heel pain or possibly navicular syndrome.

shifting

Some horses favour resting the lame hind leg continually.

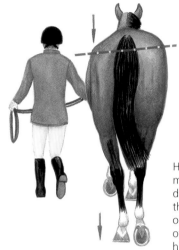

Horses may show more up and down movement through the pelvis on the lame side, often called 'hip hitching'.

How to spot hind leg lameness

In order to spot which hind leg the lameness is coming from, first of all stand your horse up square. The lame hind leg may have less musculature over that side of the pelvis. This may give you a clue as to which leg he has not been using as much, resulting in underdevelopment/loss of muscle. Also, when he is walked and trotted in a straight line, when the lame hind leg hits the ground the pelvis generally dips. In horses which are lame on both front legs or hind legs, it may be necessary to lunge them in trot on a circle, on one or both reins, in order to allow the lameness to become apparent.

Watch your horse walk and trot away and note how he carries his tail, since he may carry it crookedly, usually towards the lame side. Watch out for shifting between the hind legs, as this may indicate lameness in both hind limbs, for example arthritis in both hocks or with sacroiliac (pelvic) pain or laminitis in both hind feet.

Asymmetric pelvis with loss of gluteal muscle on left side.

Lungeing on a circle may exacerbate a limb lameness. If the pain is coming from the back or the pelvis your vet may want to see you ride the horse.

9

WHEN TO CALL THE VET

Pointing – avoiding taking weight on a front foot, e.g. in the case of a foot abscess.

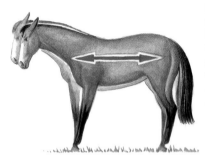

Rocking – an uncomfortable horse who is unwilling to stand and bear weight on fore or hind limbs, as seen in acute laminitis.

Injury to fetlock – the position and depth of the wound, e.g. over a joint, is more crucial than the length of the wound itself.

Kick injury below hock – a common site for a kick injury, which can result in a fracture of the splint bone.

If your horse has gone lame you may be unsure as to whether to call your vet. However, if you are in any doubt, phone him and have a chat, particularly if there is no obvious reason for the sudden onset of lameness.

There are various factors which can be considered before calling your vet and which might determine the urgency of a visit. The two most important points are: the period of lameness (how long has the horse been lame?), and how lame he is. If the lameness is mild then it may be feasible to wait a day or two to see if it gets better or worse. However, if your horse or pony is very lame and appears to be in some degree of pain, then you should call your vet straight away.

If your horse has been shod very recently and has gone lame the cause might be a tight nail or some other shoeing-related problem. Contact your farrier and discuss the recent shoeing with him. He may call in, remove the shoe and recommend either poulticing or replacing the shoe.

If you have been to a competition and your horse or pony has gone suddenly lame a day or two later this should alert you to certain possibilities. Following competitions, bruised feet, strained tendons and muscle problems are not uncommon.

Nail in frog – a crucial area of the foot which, if penetrated, can result in vital structures being damaged or infected, with grave consequences – e.g. the navicular bone or bursa, or the deep digital flexor tendon.

First, stand your horse up square, so that the front and hind legs are in an equal position. This will allow your vet to see and compare each leg separately.

How to trot up your horse correctly

It is essential to be able to trot up your horse for your veterinary surgeon or farrier, so that his action can be assessed. Your farrier may wish to check the balance of the foot whilst your horse is moving, and the veterinary surgeon may need to see the horse walked and trotted in hand to establish which is the lame leg and to see how lame he is.

Always use a bridle to do this, so you have more control, and lead him with the reins held loose (so as not to interfere with his head carriage), from his left side. Wear gloves and a hard hat, for safety reasons, since he may become excitable.

Your vet may ask you to trot the horse up two or three times, and this might be followed by making him go backwards or turn tightly in a small circle in both directions, so that he has to cross his limbs. This may also be followed by flexion tests (see page 12), so be prepared for quite a bit of running!

WALK

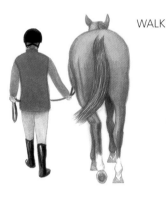

With the reins held firmly but loosely, walk in a straight line away from the vet, for approximately 20m, ensuring the horse is straight and walking forward in a positive fashion.

Turn him away from you so you remain on the outside of his body, and walk back smartly in a straight line towards your vet.

TROT

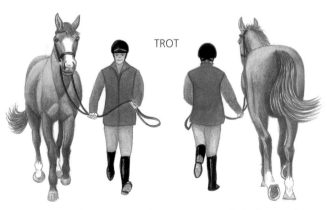

Repeat the exercise at the trot, again with the head held loose, in order that your vet can check for any movement of the head or neck.

TURN ON SMALL CIRCLE

Making a tight turn on a small circle, ensuring that the horse crosses his legs.

LAMENESS GRADING AND DIAGNOSTIC TECHNIQUES

GRADES   0/5   1/5   2/5   3/5   4/5

A horse graded 5/5 would be 'non-weightbearing lame' and not moving.

Lameness grading

Vets have developed a standardised lameness scoring system which allows them to assess lameness more accurately and consistently, on a scale of 0 to 5. This scoring system for lameness is based on their observations of horses trotting in hand in a straight line on a firm, non-slip surface.

Grade 0/5 indicates he is sound.

Grade 1/5 indicates mild lameness. If the lameness is in a foreleg there may be a slight head nod only. When the lameness is in a hind limb a slight dipping of the pelvis on the affected side may be seen.

Grade 2/5 indicates obvious lameness. Head nod and pelvic movement are seen consistently, with the head and pelvis moving several centimetres. You should call your vet.

Grade 3/5 shows pronounced head nod and dipping of the pelvis.

Grade 4/5 is consistent with severe and marked lameness. Lameness is often seen at the walk and when asked to trot the horse may show an extreme head nod or dipping of his pelvis. He may find it difficult to trot.

Grade 5/5 shows he does not want to bear any weight on the affected leg. A horse with a grade 5/5 is classified as 'non-weightbearing lame'. He should not be moved and needs immediate veterinary attention.

Flexion tests

Vets carry out flexion tests for a variety of reasons, including lameness investigation and for vettings. Horses being examined for sale are generally sound but flexion tests **may** uncover a hidden source of lameness. The limb is held up and flexed for 30–45 seconds. On releasing the leg, the horse is trotted away in a straight line and the degree of lameness and for how long it lasts is noted. If the lameness is marked and carries on for eight to twelve steps or more this may be taken as a positive response. It is important to compare both forelegs and then compare both hind legs following flexion.

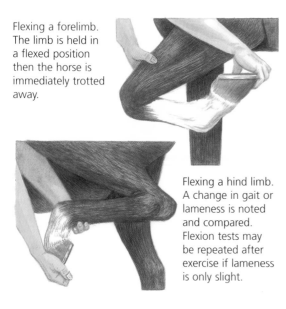

Flexing a forelimb. The limb is held in a flexed position then the horse is immediately trotted away.

Flexing a hind limb. A change in gait or lameness is noted and compared. Flexion tests may be repeated after exercise if lameness is only slight.

Use of nerve-blocks

It may be necessary to use nerve-blocks to establish which part of the leg the lameness is originating from. Vets only use nerve-blocking on a horse's leg after a thorough clinical examination, involving gait assessment, palpation of the limbs, and the use of hoof testers on the foot. If there are two areas of possible lameness in a leg, nerve-blocking is a good way of establishing which one is causing the pain. Local anaesthetic is injected under the skin in order to freeze the nerve which innervates that particular area of the leg. The vet will usually start at the lowest point and freeze (numb) in a methodical manner up the leg towards the shoulder. (It is a bit like being at the dentist when you have your tooth frozen before drilling!) By removing the pain from a certain area of the leg, the horse will appear sounder (if not completely sound), thereby telling us from which area of the leg the lameness and pain is originating.

X-rays and scans

If your vet has managed to localise an area of lameness and there is nothing obvious to see, he may decide to X-ray that area or carry out an ultrasound scan. X-rays show us the bones and joints, whereas ultrasound scans show the tendons and ligaments (soft tissues). It is now possible to carry out radioactive isotope bone scanning in order to show 'hot spots'. This is particularly useful in back and pelvic problems, e.g. sacroiliac injuries. Vets are now able to carry out MRI (magnetic resonance imaging) scans on the feet and lower limbs of horses and ponies, which can give us a more accurate image of the bones, joints and soft tissues.

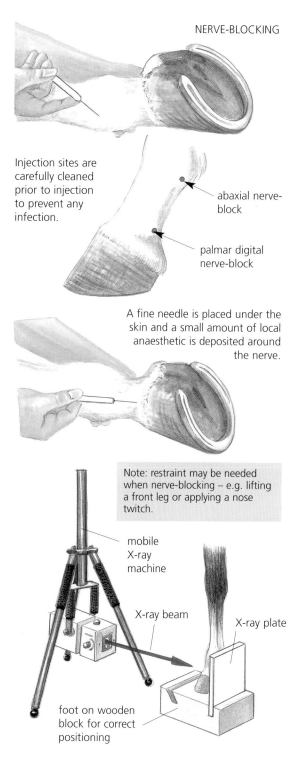

NERVE-BLOCKING

Injection sites are carefully cleaned prior to injection to prevent any infection.

abaxial nerve-block

palmar digital nerve-block

A fine needle is placed under the skin and a small amount of local anaesthetic is deposited around the nerve.

Note: restraint may be needed when nerve-blocking – e.g. lifting a front leg or applying a nose twitch.

mobile X-ray machine

X-ray beam

X-ray plate

foot on wooden block for correct positioning

Foot problems

The foot is the commonest site of lameness in horses and ponies. Although the hoof capsule is very strong and resilient, the lower part of your horse's leg is constantly being subjected to pressure, trauma and concussion. The foot, though, is not an easy structure to examine because of the rigid, outer hoof capsule. Close examination (often after removing the shoe), using a hoof knife and hoof testers is often necessary.

Signs of foot problems include increased heat in one or both feet, particularly around the front of the foot and the coronary band, an increased pulse (best felt at the back of and below the fetlock) and sensitivity to hoof testers. The most common foot-related lameness problems are: (a) foot abscesses; (b) bruising and corns; (c) nail bind or other shoeing-related lameness; and (d) sore heel syndrome.

VETERINARY EXAMINATION OF THE FOOT

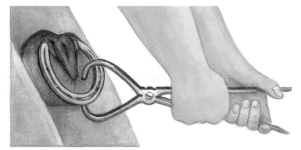

Stage one involves carefully hoof-testing the foot before shoe removal.

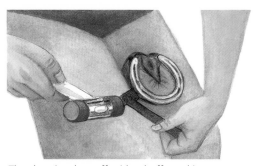

The shoe is taken off with a buffer, taking care to remove all nails and not allowing the foot to break up.

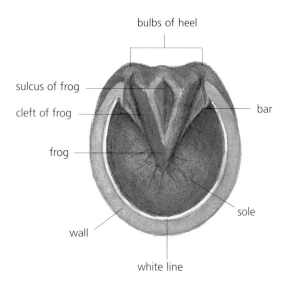

UNDERSIDE OF FOOT

bulbs of heel

sulcus of frog

cleft of frog

bar

frog

wall

sole

white line

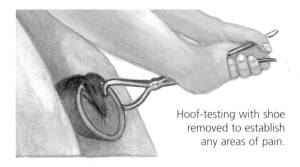

Hoof-testing with shoe removed to establish any areas of pain.

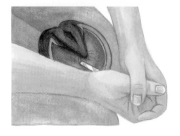

Using hoof knife to pare excess sole and debris, before examining for signs of bruising, abscesses, penetrations, etc.

14

FOOT ABSCESSES

Foot abscesses

These can result in extreme lameness in either a front or a hind foot. You may find your horse or pony has suddenly gone very lame and is unable to move or bear any weight on the limb. The most likely explanation is a foot abscess. Some horses and ponies are predisposed towards foot abscesses and they are more common when conditions are wet. The wetness weakens the hoof structure and allows infection into the foot. If your horse has a foot abscess he will almost certainly have increased heat and this is best judged by comparison with the other feet. There may also be an increased pulse at the back of the fetlock and the vein on the inside of the leg may be filled. Some horses with foot abscesses may be in such pain and distress that they break out in a sweat, pant, or lie down.

Common areas of abscess formation.

Flush infected area with iodine or dilute peroxide.

Action plan: The foot should be cleaned thoroughly and then examined. Use a hoofpick to tap the foot gently and isolate the area of pain. Vets and farriers use hoof testers. Having cleaned the foot, and found there is no obvious penetration of the sole, it may be necessary to have the shoe removed and then to pare the foot back to see where the source of the abscess is. Abscesses are common around the white line under the shoe. Horses and ponies kept on flinty ground will often have abscesses as a result of flint penetration. Once the abscess is drained you can then 'tub' your horse's foot in a bucket of warm water and Epsom salts, before applying a poultice (e.g. Animalintex). It may be necessary to carry out the tubbing and poulticing over the space of three to four days in order to draw out all the infection, and this should be continued until the hole is not discharging any pus. Depending on the position of the abscess, the whole cavity can be packed or a pad applied to the foot before the shoe is replaced. Ask your vet whether your horse or pony is up to date with his tetanus inoculation. Occasionally, antibiotics may be required to clear up a foot abscess and it may be necessary to give painkillers for two to three days in order to reduce the pain.

Tubbing in a bucket of Epsom salts and warm water to help draw out infection.

Applying a poultice (e.g. Animalintex), padding and taping to keep it all in place.

Bruised feet and corns

Bruised feet, perhaps from riding on stony or uneven ground, are common problems. Corns are also the result of bruising of the sensitive tissues of the sole in the angle between the walls and bars and may be due to concussion or inadequate heel support. If the shoe is fitted too short over the heels with inadequate length or if the horse has poor foot conformation (with low heels and a broken back hoof/pastern axis) then he may be more prone to developing corns. Also, if you leave a shoe on for too long, your horse may be more liable to problems. Regular shoeing is **very** important.

Using hoof testers it is possible to isolate the source of the bruising and pain. The shoe may need to be removed and the bruising pared away. If there is any infection then the foot will require poulticing prior to re-shoeing with a seated-out shoe (longer and wider at the heels). If there is a bad sole bruise then fitting your horse or pony's foot with a pad may be helpful. Pads can be made of either leather or plastic and may have synthetic packing between the sole and the pad to provide protection and cushioning.

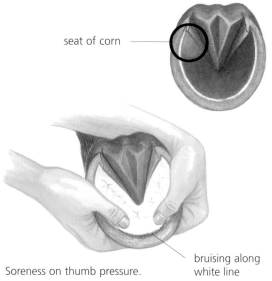

seat of corn

Soreness on thumb pressure.

bruising along white line

Foot shod with full pad. Some pads come with a frog insert or frog support. Silicone or other materials can be placed under the pad to provide cushioning and support.

Shoe too small – produces imbalance and may result in bruising in the toe region.

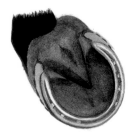

Shoe too short – will predispose this foot to the development of corns (bruising) because the branches of the shoe are pressing in the sensitive corn area.

SHOEING-RELATED PROBLEMS

A **nail bind** can occur when a nail of the shoe is driven close to the sensitive structures of the foot, resulting in inflammation and pressure. The horse may not be immediately lame following a nail bind, but the next day lameness may be apparent and getting gradually worse. If you tap the sole or wall around the offending nail this may produce a reaction. Treatment involves removing the offending nail or, if the horse is particularly lame, removing the shoe.

Nail prick occurs when the farrier's nail penetrates the sensitive structures of the foot. This is most likely to happen if your horse or pony is difficult to shoe and misbehaves whilst being shod or if his hoof walls are thin or have been broken from having lost a shoe previously. A nail prick is very painful. The shoe will have to be removed, followed by tubbing and poulticing in combination with anti-inflammatories.

Lameness can follow either **poor balancing of the horse's foot** or **inadequate shoeing** techniques. If the feet are overgrown or neglected, resulting in marked imbalance, then lameness can occur. If the toes get too long and the heels collapse then this can cause changes in the stress placed on the internal structures of the foot and the limb. To correct the imbalance, X-rays may be required to establish the position of the pedal bone inside the hoof. Your farrier may decide to change the style of shoe he uses to best suit your horse's foot. It is crucial that the foot is trimmed and balanced correctly before the correct shoe is applied. **Regular shoeing and trimming at least every 5–6 weeks is necessary.**

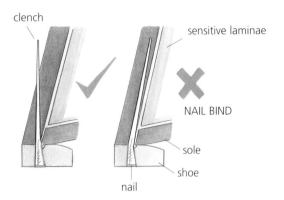

clench

sensitive laminae

NAIL BIND

sole

shoe

nail

Position of clenches in a correctly shod foot.

IMBALANCE

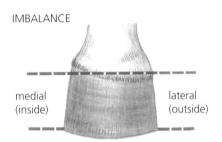

medial (inside)

lateral (outside)

The coronary band (or coronet) should be parallel to the ground (bearing surface).

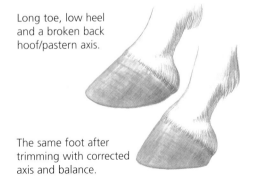

Long toe, low heel and a broken back hoof/pastern axis.

The same foot after trimming with corrected axis and balance.

SPLINTS AND BONE SPAVIN

Splints

All horses have two splint bones on each leg, running from below the knee/hock to just above the fetlock. If you find a hard swelling on your horse's leg on the outside or inside of the cannon

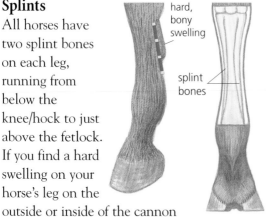

hard, bony swelling

splint bones

bone, the likelihood is that he has developed a splint. Splints can be caused through concussion, trauma or a knock and may be the result of damage to the interosseous ligament, which joins the splint bone to the cannon bone. Initially when they occur they may be hot and painful and can cause lameness. Some horses go slightly 'unlevel' just before the splint actually appears. However, once the splint is forming your horse should be rested, otherwise it might enlarge or even result in chronic lameness.

Treatment involves cold hosing (or ice packing) in combination with rest and support bandaging. Some large splints may rub on the suspensory ligament causing lameness. The horse should be restricted until all the heat and pain has gone from the leg.

Ensuring your horse has good foot balance, avoiding working on hard ground and using support bandages for exercise will go a long way to preventing splints forming.

Bone spavin

Bone spavin, an arthritic condition, affects the joints in the hocks. A spavin is usually gradual in onset and initially the lameness is often mild. However, some horses can become very lame with spavins. Poor hock conformation and hard work may predispose a horse to developing bone spavins. There may be a connection with a hereditary condition in young Warmblood horses called OCD (osteochondritis dissecans).

The hock is made up of four joint compartments and it is usually the two lower joints which are affected with osteoarthritis. Sometimes a hard, bony swelling appears on the inside of the hock. As the cartilage is eroded away in the joint the condition becomes more painful. When spavins appear in both hocks the horse may appear very stiff, rather than lame. X-rays and nerve-blocking are required to confirm the diagnosis and a treatment plan might involve remedial shoeing in combination with a controlled exercise programme with the use of anti-inflammatories (injections or powders). Eventually, with careful treatment and patience, many cases of bone spavin 'settle down' enough so that the horse can lead a reasonably normal life, even if at a lower level of performance.

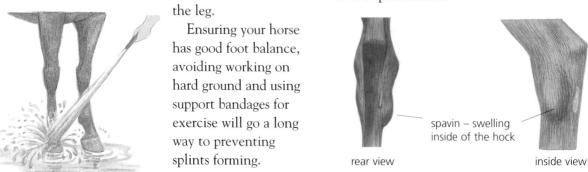

spavin – swelling inside of the hock

rear view

inside view

RINGBONE AND WOUNDS

Articular ringbone

This is an arthritic condition affecting the lower joints of the horse's leg. A common site for ringbone involves the coffin joint in the front foot. Horses may start to trip or stumble or their gait may appear shortened before they actually go lame. A change in shoeing or foot balance or an increase in the workload may predispose some horses, particularly heavier breeds, to ringbone. The lameness may be exacerbated by flexion tests and by lungeing on a circle. You may be able to detect heat and swelling just above the coronary band or in the pastern area. Diagnosis is by nerve-blocking and X-rays. Treatment involves rest in combination with anti-inflammatories. Particular attention should be paid to the balance of the foot (hoof/pastern axis) and remedial shoeing may be required to improve the breakover and increase the amount of support to the foot. Your vet and farrier will advise you.

Types of wounds causing lameness

Look for wounds on the leg and in particular any that may be near a joint or tendon sheath – for example, cuts over or near the fetlock or the knee should be watched more carefully than a superficial wound on the neck or the flank. Some small, innocuous-looking wounds over joints may have penetrated the joint itself and result in infection (or sepsis) which can be very serious. Look for clear, slightly yellowy viscous fluid – it might indicate 'joint oil' seeping from the wound. If you are worried about a wound overlying a joint or tendon sheath, cover it with a sterile (Melonin) dressing and call your vet.

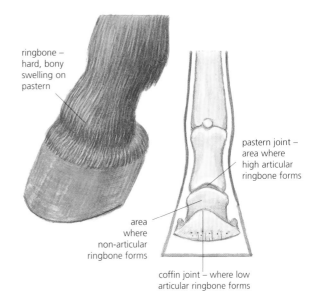

ringbone – hard, bony swelling on pastern

pastern joint – area where high articular ringbone forms

area where non-articular ringbone forms

coffin joint – where low articular ringbone forms

COMMON WOUND SITES POTENTIALLY LEADING TO SERIOUS LAMENESS

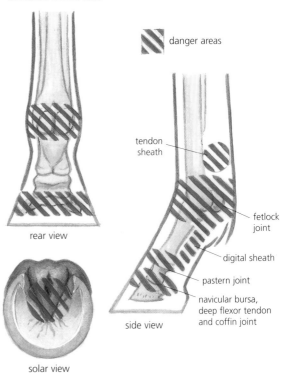

danger areas

tendon sheath

fetlock joint

digital sheath

pastern joint

navicular bursa, deep flexor tendon and coffin joint

rear view

solar view

side view

TENDON AND LIGAMENT INJURIES

Tendon injuries are a common problem in horses, particularly those jumping or working at fast speeds. They most commonly occur in one front leg and involve either the superficial or deep flexor tendon. The tendon acts to join the muscle onto the bone and serves to transmit any forces. If under undue pressure or fatigue, this stretches, and once beyond a certain limit this results in fibre tearing and damage (tendonitis). This produces heat, pain and swelling. Mild cases may show only slight heat and swelling and very little lameness. With more severe tendon damage the symptoms can be more dramatic, and some horses appear very lame. Once the damaged tendon has healed this leaves a degree of thickening and if excessive this is known as 'bowed tendons'. Treatment involves strict rest in combination with cold hosing at regular intervals and bandaging. It may be necessary to give the horse anti-inflammatories/painkillers to reduce the swelling and pain. Many tendon injuries take six to twelve months or even longer to heal, particularly when badly damaged. The latest tendon treatment technology involves the use of stem cell therapy. It may be useful to ultrasound scan the tendon to establish the extent of the injury and to form a prognosis as to the outcome. Re-scanning at regular intervals allows us to monitor the healing process and gauge when the horse may be most likely to start walking exercise and then resume normal work.

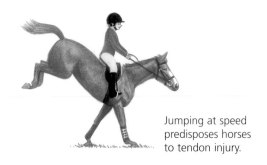

Jumping at speed predisposes horses to tendon injury.

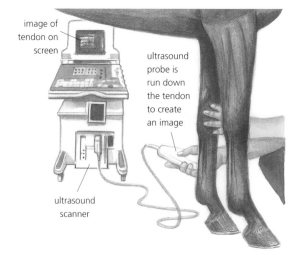

bowed tendon – enlarged superficial flexor tendon due to torn or damaged fibres

Suspensory ligaments are also vulnerable to damage, can result in lameness and may take up to 12–14 months to heal satisfactorily.

ULTRASOUND SCANNING

image of tendon on screen

ultrasound probe is run down the tendon to create an image

ultrasound scanner

LAMINITIS

Laminitis is a very painful condition affecting one or more feet, and is particularly common in ponies turned out on unrestricted pasture. There are many causes of laminitis, including excessive feed intake (particularly grass), trauma, infection, and medical conditions such as Cushing's disease.

Typical stance of a pony with laminitis.

The hoof capsule is rigid and when there is increased blood flow to the feet, the blood vessels become engorged and result in extreme pain. This may also lead to the dying off of normal healthy tissue, which destabilises the pedal bone. The pedal bone may lose its support structure and either sink or rotate in a downwards direction.

Laminitis should always be regarded as an emergency and you must call your vet immediately. The vet will start a treatment programme involving removal of the cause, in combination with box rest, attention to foot support and pain relief. Many cases of laminitis, if caught early enough, can respond quickly. However, if secondary complications have taken place, particularly in the feet, then treatment may be very prolonged and expensive, with poor results. Often ponies with laminitis will spend more time lying down or have difficulty in turning in either direction and this should alert you immediately to the possibility of this problem.

Action plan: Remove your pony from the pasture and put him in a stable filled with a deep shavings bed. His diet, which must be closely regulated and monitored, should consist of mainly hay in combination with some high-fibre feed twice a day. Your vet will give the pony pain relief, and apply frog supports to the feet. All treatment is directed at preventing irreversible changes in the feet taking place. Once your pony has had laminitis, he will be more prone to developing it in the future. If he doesn't appear to respond well, or is suffering from a particularly bad attack of laminitis, it may be necessary to take X-rays of his feet to establish the position of the pedal bone in the foot, before the farrier is able to carry out remedial shoeing. Recuperation can take many months of nursing and care, with particular attention being paid to feed intake, exercise and shoeing. Certain ponies appear to be more prone to developing laminitis – however, if they are exercised regularly, in combination with dietary management, this may go a long way to prevention.

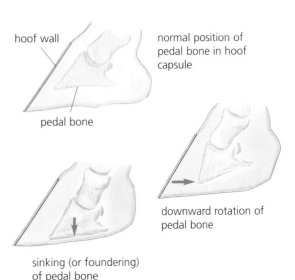

hoof wall

pedal bone

normal position of pedal bone in hoof capsule

downward rotation of pedal bone

sinking (or foundering) of pedal bone

MUSCLE PROBLEMS

'Tying-up' (Rhabdomyolosis)

With heavy exercise some horses are prone to 'tying-up'. This is similar to cramp in people and is due to excess lactic acid in the muscles. It is a very painful condition and some horses are unable to move. If tying up occurs while out riding, dismount immediately and remove  the saddle. It is better not to move the horse unless necessary, and call for help. He should be returned to his yard in a low-loading trailer. Once home he should be well rugged up, given a bran mash (in order to prevent the onset of colic) and have his legs bandaged. This is an emergency and in moderate and severe cases your vet should be called. The vet will administer an anti-inflammatory and painkillers to make the horse feel more comfortable, and may take a blood sample to measure the muscle enzymes CK and AST (which will confirm muscle damage).

Most horses make a good recovery with changes in the diet, increased turn-out, a controlled work programme, along with electrolyte supplementation.

Pulled Muscles (Myositis)

Horses and ponies are very susceptible to pulling muscles either from playing around and slipping in the field or through strenuous exercise. The muscles most commonly affected are those in the back and the pelvis; however, muscles in the neck and fore- and upper hind limbs can also be damaged or inflamed.

If your horse pulls a muscle in his back or his quarters he may be very sore and resent the saddle being fitted, or being ridden. Once your vet has examined him and diagnosed the problem he may recommend physiotherapy, in combination with rest. One common cause of pulled muscles in horses and ponies is lack of fitness. In order to prevent muscle problems, horses should always be got fit gradually, including four to six weeks of slow walking exercise. Before you school or jump (or undertake any serious exercise with) your horse make sure that he is well warmed up by walking him for ten to fifteen minutes beforehand. Avoid sudden over-exertion in order to prevent muscle strain. After exercise always 'warm down' to ensure recovery.

Checking for soreness in the back by gently palpating the muscles either side of the midline.

PREVENTING LAMENESS

Regular shoeing. Don't be tempted to extend the shoeing interval beyond the normal length (usually four to six weeks). It may be tempting to cut costs in this way but it will definitely predispose your horse or pony to foot problems, including sore heels, navicular syndrome and bruising.

Before riding, and preferably on a daily basis, be sure to **pick out your horse's feet** thoroughly. A stone or flint that has become wedged between the shoe and frog may result in sole penetration and abscesses forming. If your horse has flattish feet and thin soles you should be extra vigilant. When riding, avoid stony tracks and, if you have to use them, do so only in walk. Consider fitting pads.

Ensure your horse is fit enough for the work you expect of him. Hacking for two to three hours can be extremely hard work, particularly over uneven and hilly terrain. You should spend two months in a slow, gradual fittening programme before taking part in any sponsored rides or long hacks. Walk at the start and finish of all exercise.

Nutrition. Only horses competing at high levels require high-energy feeds. For general riding, most horses will have enough energy if they are fed good-quality hay in combination with high-fibre nuts and possibly a non-heating mix, as well as minerals and vitamins. If your horse sweats a lot or if the weather is very hot, it may be worthwhile feeding him electrolytes on a daily basis, particularly if he is prone to metabolic or tying-up problems. If he has poor quality feet (poor quality or flaky horn) discuss feeding supplements that might improve the quality of the feet with your vet or farrier. Access to fresh water is necessary at all times.

Always fit some form of **leg protection** while exercising, particularly on the front legs to protect the tendons, splint and cannon bones from injury. Likewise, while travelling use full-limb bandages from the knees and hocks down, or travelling boots. This will go a long way to preventing self-inflicted injury, wounds and abrasions of the lower limbs, which can result in lameness or infection.

If you are changing fields or yards take care when introducing new horses or ponies. Horses are generally best kept in pairs. Separate geldings and mares to prevent kick injuries. Removing hind shoes will reduce the risk of serious injuries.

Finally, check your horse's legs regularly for signs of heat, pain and swelling and compare one limb against the other. Any changes may alert you to potential lameness.

BOX REST

When is box rest necessary?

As a general rule, if your horse or pony is lame at the walk, he should be confined to a box or small yard until the lameness resolves and he shows a marked improvement. This will ensure that if the cause of lameness is serious he does no further damage. If your vet has to remove the shoe to treat an abscess or a bruised foot, confinement may be necessary to prevent any further trauma or damage (e.g. loss of wall) before your farrier can put the shoe back on.

If your horse has sustained a serious tendon or ligament injury, then prolonged box or yard rest may be necessary to allow the damaged area to heal satisfactorily without added pressure of exercise and further damage.

Horses on box rest should be feed a diet that is high in fibre and low in protein. Horses have relatively small stomachs and require small amounts of feed, often. The bulk of the diet should comprise good quality hay (soaked if necessary), some high-fibre nuts or chaff (in order to prevent boredom) and a plentiful supply of fresh water. A small feed twice a day may be necessary in order to give medication.

Most horses and ponies will resign themselves to box rest. Keep stress to a minimum, by allowing him to see a companion and developing a regular routine, for example regular feed times. Regular grooming is very important, as is attending to his feet. Ensure they are picked out and cleaned thoroughly.

Certain problems may result through lack of movement, for example, filled legs (and sheath in geldings) and loss of muscle (topline). If the hind legs start to swell it might be helpful to massage his legs twice a day and apply stable bandages in order to keep the legs warm and to improve the circulation.

Horses on box rest should have a deep, even bed and stable bandages on all four legs to prevent swelling and improve comfort.

Minimum stable size should be 12ft x 12ft (3.6m x 3.6m), preferably 12ft x 16ft (3.6m x 4.8m).

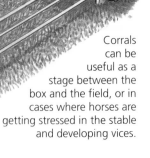

Corrals can be useful as a stage between the box and the field, or in cases where horses are getting stressed in the stable and developing vices.